From Across the Universe

The Sunrise becomes personal

Conrad Ziegler

Published by The Lighthouse books, Agape Inc.

For more information regarding permission, write to:
The Lighthouse Books, 13721 E. Rice Pl, Aurora,
CO 80015.

The pictures used in the book were taken by Conrad Ziegler.
ISBN: 978-1-950320-53-0 [Paperback]
ISBN: 978-1-950320-51-6 [Digital]

Visit us at:
www.thelighthousebooks.com
Printed in the USA

Dedication

To Jan, who went far beyond the call of duty, and into the realm of sacrificial love. I will never be able to thank you enough for what you did. Forever in your debt, and knowing I will be, forever.

To Jane, whose loving service to me while recuperating not only provided what I needed but hastened my recovery.

To Joe, whose big heart kept me from having to go to rehab, which was huge.

To Steve, who got me through the next trauma.

Contents

Preface v

Chapter 1: No Two Sunrises Alike 2

Chapter 2: How I Got Here 3

Chapter 3: The Plan Unfolds 6

Chapter 4: The Ordeal 9

Chapter 5: The ICU 11

Chapter 6: The Intensive Care Unit Intensifies......................................14

Chapter 7: Bats in the Belfry...16

Chapter 8: Give Me Liberty or Give Me Death 20

Chapter 9: Leaving the ICU 22

Chapter 10: The Chaplain 24

Chapter 11: Coming Home..28

Chapter 12: New Beginning...31

Chapter 13: The First Night Home...34

Chapter 14: Cords..36

Chapter 15: The Sun Also Rises..40

Chapter 16: The Sun Also Rises..42

Chapter 17: From Across the Universe 46

Chapter 18: My First Sunrise 61

Epilogue 65

Preface

Sunrise. A symbol of hope.
A symbol of Christian hope.

While it is true that Christianity is not the only group or culture that considers the sunrise a symbol of hope, for Christians the connection is a special one. It is special because it is very personal.

The sun rises, from the night.

The Son rose, from the dead.

Jesus made some important promises. Through His death and resurrection, we were to be blessed, not only in this life but in life into eternity. He died, so that we might live.

It is no accident, or empty tradition, that every Easter there are "sunrise" services all over the world. A beautiful symbol of our hope is combined with a very personal reason for that hope.

After surviving a double surgery, I came home weak and emaciated. Pain and I mean pain that's hard to describe. I had rejected the use of strong pain medication because of the side effects, some serious enough to terrify me in the ICU. But enduring some relentless pain wasn't my biggest problem.

Because of the nature of the surgeries, I had a different body. My heart was different, my chest was very different, and my brain, being at least half missing, had difficulty with all three changes. Hard to describe, but my brain couldn't grasp the implications of the changes. Not only aware of loss but what was there felt like somebody else. My rebuilt chest and heart felt alien to me. My damaged brain just added to that feeling. Sort of mimicking a Twilight Zone episode, I felt like I was in a different dimension, with everything slightly changed. The word 'alien' popped into my consciousness often.

It didn't help that when I first returned home, I was afraid to look at my naked self in the mirror. I knew that when I did look, I would think, "That's not me." In a world where I was already having identity issues, this was not good.

I needed hope that I would find myself. Or maybe, I needed hope that I could accept myself in what I had become. So, I started walking, in search of it.

At first, I was too weak to do much. I could only drag my huge oxygen canister behind me around the block. A small block.

As I got stronger, I decided sunrise was the best time to go. And I walked into my first sunrise. That morning, in pursuit of freedom? Identity? Breath of life? My reason for this pursuit was unknown, still, I walked, and I saw my very first sunrise. I was transfixed; it was truly beautiful.

While I had noticed sunrises before, maybe even commented on them to whomever was nearby, I had never really seen one. I had never, ever absorbed one. Until then. I could feel a small bit of strength returning to my body.

Some sunrises were pretty, some were stunning, and some were muted. But most of the time, they made a statement, maybe even started a story…

I wanted to remember, so, I started to take pictures.

Here, is a very important part of my journey of recovery, not only of my body but of myself. Every morning is another way to gaze at the heavens and be reminded of the hope that is within us.

I had a dream in the ICU, most likely opiate. I dreamt I was on a South Pacific Island, with waterfalls, lush greenery, and tropical birds making the most wonderful music. This picture, which I took four months later, three blocks from my house, had some similarities to it.

CHAPTER 1

No Two Sunrises Alike

It has been said that no two snowflakes are alike. Same with sunrises. Even in dry, windless periods, with the expansion of the eastern plains as a backdrop, no two sunrises are exactly alike. Even when they look similar, there's always a difference (from the same perspective). Every day, because of the rotation of the earth, the sun comes up either three degrees (depending upon the time of year) north, or even three degrees south of the day before. That makes the horizon change, even if it's ever-so-little, along with changes in the air and wisps of clouds.

This only adds to the great diversity of sunrises we already have, in Colorado. Because of the dryness of the climate, we wake up to fewer cloudy, or foggy mornings. In climates like this, our passionate artist paints pictures so varied that one could fill up art galleries all over the world just by sitting or walking in Aurora.

Every morning.

(Note: Some of the pictures in this book will not be of directly looking into the sun. Some will be looking the opposite way, showing the sunrises' effects on the morning…)

CHAPTER 2

How I Got Here

Why would anybody start "seeing" sunrises for the first time in their life, at age 67? A better question would be, why did it take so long?

One evening early last year, I went to bed not feeling well. My breathing was a bit labored, and my feet were slightly swollen. Looking in the mirror, I saw bloodshot eyes. While the breathing issue bothered me, I didn't feel sick in any other way, so, I just went to bed.

I woke up the next morning, and my breathing had become more difficult. My feet were so swollen that I could barely see my toes. Walking was difficult. My eyes looked as though they were filled with blood. This scared me.

Uh-oh.

Struggling to get dressed, my breathing was labored and worsening with each breath. *Forget about breakfast.*

I wondered if I should call someone. "No time," I thought to myself. Even though my worsening breathing made my movements slow, I tried my best to quickly make it to my car.

Fifteen minutes and thirteen blocks later, I literally crawled into the ER.

"I..... can't........breathe.........." was all I could rasp.

This was at the height of Covid, so fortunately, they were ready with the oxygen.

I remember trying to calculate how many seconds I had left to live once they put the oxygen on me.

After testing me with some poking, prodding, and pinching, I waited in an ER bed for a couple of hours. Then, the news came. What was happening to me wasn't Covid, but they were putting me in the hospital anyway. Something about heart failure and looking for surgeons. The word 'surgeon' alone, got my attention. The plural, 'surgeons', gave me pause.

I just had this little, itty-bitty feeling deep down inside, that my life as I had known it, was over.

I wasn't really aware of this at the time, but it was going to be quite a while until I saw a sunrise again.

In the middle of my life, I found myself in a dark wood, for the straightway was lost.
- Dante, The Divine Comedy

CHAPTER 3

The Plan Unfolds

My health has been good enough that I seldomly ever saw a doctor, other than a yearly check-up. The only time I ever ventured into a hospital, was when I was visiting others. I visited my wife in the hospital every day, for six months, until she passed away.

My wife had made the most of it, cruising around every day on the 8th floor with her walker and IVs. She was getting to know, personally, every nurse on the floor and the names of their children and spouses. Never, ever complained. This was harder on me than it was on her because I hated to even be in a hospital. I felt no small amount of shame over that.

I had three deep-seated fears in my life, and two of them were about to come true. *The first one had already come true, to my lasting grief.* I was deathly afraid of open-heart surgery. Whenever I caught a glimpse of it on TV or heard somebody telling me about an open-heart "procedure", my mind would rush into a scene of my chest being slit open, with no anesthesia, baring all my interior organs where surgeons would start cutting again, with unbridled glee. This vision would always start making my knees knock.

And needles.

When I was nine years old, I received a tetanus shot in my arm. It felt so bad, and the sight of the huge needle diving into my person was so horrifying, that for a few moments, the adrenaline rush kept me standing. Proudly thinking I had conquered a world, I headed back to my classroom and passed out before I got to the door. When I came to, I felt bad, and have shrunk back from needles ever since.

In the present day, I found myself in a hospital room with oxygen coming from a wall, two IVs in my arm, and nurses drawing blood, it seemed, every hour. I got to learn all about pic-lines. Needles and pic-lines would be my constant companion for the next sixteen days.

I was a pure prisoner. Not really understanding my plight, all I could think of was, "When do I get out?" Of course, I would quit with that pipedream as soon as the surgeons and their assistants started to arrive, explaining very carefully my near future.

One would repair a mitral valve in my heart, which had fallen almost completely off, hanging by a thread, literally. I had been living with an open valve for a couple of years that had caused some minor problems with low blood pressure and bouts of light-headedness, but that was it. My cardiologist had told me that some people have lived with this for years if things didn't change. Well, they did change. My valve was unhinged on one side, hanging by a thread on the other. I would need open-heart surgery to sew the valve back on.

But that was only half of it.

A thoracic surgeon explained to me what he was going to do. He told me about the Ravitch procedure. To be done at the same time as the open-heart surgery.

Years earlier, my family doctor suggested that I get this "procedure" done. Because of the chest deformity, I was born with, Pectus Excavatum, my lungs, and to a lesser degree, my heart, were being pressed in by my ribcage. It was causing COPD in my lungs and was doing my heart no favors. At that time, I was feeling fine, so I did not listen to my doctor.

To make the complicated simple, the Ravitch is a "procedure" where the surgeon does not break every bone in the chest, only the important ones. This is to be able to move the chest up and away from the interior organs, which it is no longer protecting, but squashing.

This breaking of bones and moving of the chest would take place at the same time as the open-heart surgery. A medical marvel.

Oh, joy. When do we get started?

Because of the tender mercy of our God, with which the sunrise from on high shall visit us....
Luke 1:78

CHAPTER 4

The Ordeal

～

I woke up in the Recovery Room, almost nine hours later. Doubtful that I was aware that I had just been through a double surgery. Doubtful, because I was barely aware of anything. Drifting through space, but there were no stars. How could this be? Then I heard the booming voice.

"Open your eyes!"

I was so 'unaware,' that I initially did not realize my eyes were closed. I guess this is why I saw no stars.

"Open your eyes!" a louder, more insistent voice said. Then, he really got my attention.

"Conrad, open your eyes!" *It was Conrad! He was talking (yelling, it seemed) to me, Conrad.*

I tried, I really tried. After what seemed like hours of Herculean effort, I finally, finally, got one eye open. Barely. Then, the other eye opened. Barely. Each eye was now about a quarter open. Light. Sensitive. Ow. I could barely make out the yeller, who seemed to be standing a long, long, way away. I finally got both eyes cranked up to about half open. *Why were my ears so sensitive?*

The effort was tiring. Now I knew why he was shouting so. He was at least 50 yards away, at the end of a long, long room. I tried to ask him to come closer, but couldn't, because well, I couldn't talk. I tried to open my mouth, and I couldn't do it. It was then that I realized why I couldn't open my mouth. My mouth was already opened, jammed with tubes. Fatigued jaws, and pain in my throat. This was tiring, too.

I had to close my eyes because I couldn't keep them open.

But he was insistent. This went on for a year or two (in reality, it was probably a few minutes) and finally, I cranked it up. I got both eyes almost three-quarters open.

Then the picture changed. He had moved to the foot of my bed, where he always had been. *That's why he seemed so loud. Uh-oh.*

I had no idea what combining copious amounts of anesthesia and opioids would do to my brain. But, for a while at least, 80 to 90% of my brain was, I don't know, missing.

I was only vaguely aware that I should like to have that 80 to 90% back. In my state, putting complex ideas together, such as 'missing' and 'percentage' was way too challenging. I had bigger fish to fry. I was beginning to wonder why I couldn't move. As in, anything. Other than my eyelids.

CHAPTER 5

The ICU

The trip from the recovery room to the ICU was long and tedious. I was strapped in tightly so that nothing in my newly made chest and heart would move.

The claustrophobia I had begun to feel in the recovery room began to increase--even though I was being moved slowly through a hallway, it was increasing because, I had woken up just enough to realize that I was a prisoner, and would continue to be, for the unforeseeable future. *Whoo-boy! This is a fine mess you've gotten yourself into, Ollie.* I had two seven-inch titanium bars in my chest to anchor everything, yet, they weren't completely set yet, either. Why I was thinking about this at this time, I'm not sure. Maybe some part of my chest had moved, as it would often in the months to come, but it would take months for the cartilage in my chest to completely heal. In the meantime, just heal, baby.

With my oxygen tank in tow, and my IV bottles extended above my head, anchored to the bed that had to be kept stable, it was a slow and arduous journey.

Time was warped, unreal. The trip to the ICU probably took about twenty minutes, at best. But to my anesthetized brain, and my windowless eyes, it seemed as if the trip took hours. I think I even wondered, at the time, if they were taking me to another hospital. I finally ended up in what would be my home for the next seven days, the ICU. I had no idea it would be this noisy. Nurses, God bless them, hurrying everywhere, electronic screens, wires, and tubes were everywhere. Noises. Things being dropped, beeping, and instructions thrown seemingly everywhere. It felt like I was in an Altman movie. Cacophony. Some noises jolted me, had I been able to move, lights hurting my eyes. *Have to close them. Can't sleep here, for sure. Too much.*

Finally, things quieted down. About this time, the lights were dimmed. Quiet. Better. Then, someone on the other side of a curtain began to gasp, wheeze, choke, and cough. Sounded bad. Rushing footsteps and a call for help caused another nurse and doctor to rush in. Commands barked out, electronic beeps, more commands. Then quiet. Hushed medical discussion. "Stay close, I'm going to get..." More footsteps. Then quiet. Eerily so.

Just about the time I was going to start cheering for his peace and quiet, I heard a groan. Then a louder groan. Then, choking, a gasp, and then the death rattle. I had heard one before when I was at bedside when a friend had died. It was unmistakable. I was too familiar. Strangely enough, I was happy for him. His suffering was over.

Dose-of-reality-time. Mine was just beginning. There are not many experiences more difficult to come to grips with. You may be happy for the recently departed, but the way I felt, it was easy for me to wonder if I might be next. I found myself strangely short on the will-to-live idea. I had an idea why, but that really didn't matter. What could be worse than laying in the ICU with will-to-life issues?

He causes his sun to rise on the evil and the good and sends rain on the righteous and unrighteous.

Matthew 5:45

CHAPTER 6

The Intensive Care Unit Intensifies

The first night finally ended. That night, which had seemed like a week, I had not slept. The lights came on and the extra curtains over the walkways were opened. A new shift nurse came in and, while taking some more blood from me asked, "How's the pain?" I had begun to talk a little bit more by then, the anesthesia and opioids had completely worn off, and most of me was free to move around in my bed, even to adjust it up or down. My shackles were off. I then told her there were some very strange things going on in my chest, as if parts of it were moving, and frankly, some of the movement was quite painful. Some of it felt heart-related. She then told me she'd be back, after making some rounds, with some more "meds." She came back a while later and started shooting some juice into me. I think more opioids. Fast-acting, I was feeling no pain for most of the morning. It was nice to be able to talk again, even though my throat was still sore from the tubes, the "meds" took care of most of it. I had this little, tiny voice sneak into my bed, and then up into my brain that wanted to make a funny, to say, "Life is good." I quickly stifled it, as I realized the tenuousness of my situation, and that, if I uttered this out loud, I may be getting a visit from the house shrink.

I should have been sleeping by then but could not. They had noticed this. I kept closing my eyes, but every time I came close to falling asleep, my head would jerk forward, and my eyes would fly open. Now, there was plenty of noise, interruptions, and somewhat strange going's on around me to help me stay awake. Plus, frankly, at this point, I was afraid to fall asleep. For some reason, I was very concerned about not waking up. One part of me was hoping for death, but a much larger part of me wanted to be there when it happened. This caused no small amount of conflict in my drug-addled, post-anesthesia consciousness. Heart new, hurting chest, new, hurting brain, mostly gone, but waking up to strange paths. Anguish may not be an accurate description of what I was feeling, but I was looking for a way to flee reality and couldn't figure out how. The prisoner was hemmed in, on all sides.

The second nightfall happened. I think I had another large dose of "meds" late afternoon. Later came "sundown", as in, the curtains drawn, and the lights dimmed. And it was quieter. I told them I wanted no sleeping medication, as I had a bad feeling about combining that with my pain "meds." My nurse nodded her head, but I think she gave me something, anyway.

She was quite concerned. She kept telling me I had to get some real sleep.

I am not sure how much I had been sleeping. I do know it wasn't near as much as I was supposed to get. I am not sure of exactly what she gave me before lights out that night. I am not even sure what caused the following. All I know is that, soon after lights out, I began to hallucinate.

CHAPTER 7

Bats in the Belfry

Lights were dimmed, darkened. The heavy entryway curtain was closed. The second night.

To anybody's knowledge, I had not actually slept yet. Not since I had been "out" for 9-10 hours in surgery, and the recovery room. They were getting worried about me, insisting on more sleep medication, I seem to remember giving in but only accepting the smallest possible dose. I would be OK with a little. Right?

Not long after lights out, I noticed something a little eerie. The heavy curtain that had been drawn for the night was about a foot short of reaching the floor. Because of that, I could see a reflection of light coming in from the nurse's station. Every time a doctor or nurse walked by, that reflection was very quickly blocked, just for a very split-second. Split-second darkness.

Out of the corner of my eye, I thought I saw something in that split-second darkness move, out of the darkness. Wha-what? Now, I had to keep looking. Another nurse walked by. This time I saw what was moving. A bat flew right out of the quick shadow. Soundlessly, it sped toward me, and at the last second, veered over my head. My whole body jerked, as I was sure it was going for my hair. I started to involuntarily jerk my hand up, in protection. My right hand, where, luckily, I had only an unused pie-line to not tear open, raised, and fell quickly.

Where'd the bat go? I hastily "scanned the skies", as it were, turning my head every which way possible. The first jerk had gotten my nurse's attention (through a window portal where she could observe while watching my monitor). She was slowly dragging herself away from the monitor when she noticed my head swiveling around when I was supposed to be fast asleep. She came flying. As she stepped into that reflected light to open the curtain, it went quick-dark again. In just that split-second, another bat flitted out. This one turned and headed down the corridor-thank God.

"What's going on?" she asked, concern flying out of her mouth.

"Oh, not much. Say, do you happen to have a bat problem here?"

"A what?"

"Oh, ah, well, never mind." On some level, I knew I was hallucinating, but getting that part of my brain to recognize it was difficult. She said, quite sternly, "I'm going to get you some heavier sleep meds. I'll be back in a few." She knew my lack of quality sleep was a growing problem.

I do not know how long she was gone. Five minutes? Maybe. I really didn't know. But, to me, with what happened next, it would seem like five hours. Enough time, it seems to visit another world.

I think I was in a state where I was so tired that I had to close my eyes. For a while, I was in the realm between sleep and awake, but in neither.

I was transported to the nether world.

Oh, my.

I found myself in a place that was quite dark, with some small fires burning off in the distance. They looked like piles of leaves burning, dotting a very dark countryside. There were many of them, all separate, and a distance away, giving off a faint smell. *Oh, no, no, no, no! I know that smell. I had smelled it when I was hit by lightning many years ago; that of burning hair and burning flesh.*

I was in Hell.

Get. Me. Out. Get me out of here! Ple-e-e-e-ase!

Then it came out of the darkness. A dark shape, smallish, as if riding on a quiet, jet-fueled broomstick, dark, and smelling of evil. Pure evil. It flitted right past my ear, this close, and whispered, "Heh-heh-heh." Softly, while reeking of dead things. The word 'terrified' is not quite enough, here.

No escape. It had me pinned down, then made a big circle. I could barely see its outline. If not for the background fires, I couldn't see at all, and it looked like it was circling back toward me!

It was then that my nurse, very firmly, grabbed my shoulder and brought me back. Temporarily stunned, I had a hard time answering when she asked, "Are you OK?" I couldn't answer right away, she must have seen the look of terror on my face. She made a quick move for either sedation or help, I do not know. It was then that I rasped out, "I just got back from Hell."

She stopped in her tracks. She turned back to me and said, "I believe it."

For some reason, this settled me down. Which settled her down, too.

She then pulled out a rather large-looking needle, and said, "It's time for sleepy bye."

"You need to sleep", she said.

Ya know, I couldn't agree more, but the night was still young.

Every day I walk myself into a state of well-being and walk away from every illness. I have walked myself into my best thoughts, and I know of no thought so burdensome that I cannot walk away from it.

Soren Kierkegaard

Note to chapter 7

I have little doubt these hallucinations were just that.

And then again, maybe not.

Because of the clarity and intensity of the experience, I still often recall it in its entirety. Either voluntarily, or involuntary, I do not know.

Hearing. Sight. Smell. Plus, the sixth sense. All these were involved. The combination was powerful. The evil I felt was palpable, so much so, that for a short time, I felt immersed in it. Logic and reason tell me it was pure hallucination. After all, I had just experienced some bats in the belfry. Yet, there is, and always will be a very small corner of my mind that says, "what if?"

CHAPTER 8

Give Me Liberty or Give Me Death

I soon drifted off into a deep sleep. No longer fighting it, and with enough "meds" in me to sink a small boat, I went quickly into the land of pleasantries: blue skies, still water of a pond, green grass, contoured green, well-cut, shaded trees nearby. Smells of honeysuckle, jasmine, and cut grass. Robins chirping. Seemed like I was there for a long time. It was so, so soothing.

Then, bam!

The lights explode. People running. Someone yells, "His heart stopped!"

That is what I heard. She had actually said, "He quit breathing!" Someone started to move my bed. *Oh no! NO!* The doctor rushed in, barking out orders, loudly and frantically. A crowd surrounded me, and the light was blocked. *What are you all doing?* My throat is so parched that I can't speak. They hadn't moved me very far, but I was sure that they were going to. Then it hit me, they're going to take me back for more surgery. Hands everywhere touched this, grabbed that. Tubes. Then, someone appeared with a large something that looked like they were covering me up…for a trip?

No! No! No! I CAN'T go back for more surgery! My mouth opened, but I couldn't say anything, only rasping came out. Tube jammed down my throat. *You can't do this! I won't let you cut me open again! Haven't you seen my chest? It looks like a landmine went off on it, and it hurts! I won't survive another surgery!*

In reality, they had only moved my bed a few feet, so that extra aides could be close.

I tried to pray. Frantically. Nothing would come out. Physically, I could only rasp. Mentally, I was so waking-shocked that I couldn't even formulate a prayer. This was it. I felt utterly and completely forsaken. *They can't put me back there. This time they'll see me in half!* Then I started to yell. In my brokenness, for I was broken, I rasped, "Kill me! Kill me! Don't take me back! Don't. Please. Kill me first!"

For just a second, all activity around me stopped.

At the same exact moment, when all the activity had stopped and I thought I was going to pass out, I rasped what I thought was my last breath, "But You knew you weren't forsaken… I don't!!!!"

The bad news is, when I came to, I had a very sore throat with an ugly tube-like instrument in it. The good news, I was still in my home, the ICU. Of course, I hadn't been moved very far at all, and of course, I wasn't heading back to surgery. But I did not know that until now.

However, someone had heard enough to summon a chaplain to my hospital room, the minute I left ICU.

CHAPTER 9

Leaving the ICU

Seven days. And seven nights. Time. I look back at it now. I had lost all track of time. 'Day' could mean a week or two, or an hour or two. I had no idea.

It didn't help that when I first arrived in the ICU, I wasn't eating, or sleeping much, if at all. Feeling like a vegetable, with tubes keeping me alive.

After a few days, I felt strong enough to start taking walks around the ICU, and beyond.

With a helper of course and a walker, too. I was finally convinced that I would not die there. Amid the walking, I started to improve measurably. I got the news that I would be moved to a hospital room within a day or two. I would have jumped for joy, had I been able to jump. Never did the news of going to a hospital room sound so good.

One more trial before I left: I was starting to eat, and due to the nature of the surgical and post-surgical drugs I became seriously constipated on the last day. Extremely painful. Anybody who has been through surgery and ICUs knows what I'm talking about. After a great emergency mess was created, let's just say I was happy to be leaving it behind. Pardon the pun.

Never so happy to see a nice, large, hospital room, with a window! Never mind that all I could see was a brick wall, the side of the next building five yards away.

What I could see was reflected sunlight coming off the wall. Yay! Enough of the Martian winter! I'm on earth, and the sun is out there somewhere!

Doesn't that saying go, "you don't know what you got 'till it's gone?"

I thought, for a second, there was a radio on. I couldn't walk without help, but I had a room with a view!

I was so happy to be here, that I could hardly contain myself. I even started to enjoy food. Plus, I was looking forward to my first shower in many days. They had promised me. And that involved the help of my new and quite pretty hospital nurse.

The shower was enjoyable. I was even able to have the IVs unhooked while getting cleaned. This was really big. I had been tethered for at least two weeks, and it seemed a lifetime ago. In some ways, it was. I had drainage tubes and cups coming out of my chest, spotted with fresh gashes. I was emaciated, having lost 22 pounds, and my color was shockingly white. Nonetheless, I happily assured my nurse that someday soon, I would become serious marriage material again, maybe even a hot property. I even did my best Steve McQueen imitation (Papillion), and said, after getting toweled off, "How-how-how do I look?"

Nurses have a tough job. They seldom, if ever, get to laugh. But I had her laughing hard enough that I think tears were starting to come. Just making her laugh as she did, made me feel even better.

She was to keep a close eye on me, and she did. Taking measurements of my blood, oxygen, heart, brain, drainage tubes, pulse, and even nasal checks; she was busy. Food, as much as I could handle. We ended up talking quite a bit, at least much more than usual.

She noticed that I was getting a little self-conscious about the hilarity in the shower. For some reason, I started to apologize for my ill-timed bravado. She said, amidst a couple of chuckles, "Ya know, I think you are good marriage material."

God bless her heart. That didn't just make my day, it made my month.

CHAPTER 10

The Chaplain

❧

I had forgotten about the Chaplain.

When I had first been moved from the ICU to my luxury hospital suite, the greeting nurse had, after getting me settled, mentioned that the hospital Chaplain was coming to see me; sounded important. I sort of remembered some of the things I had said back in the ICU, (like begging for death when I thought they were taking me back to surgery), but I thought, maybe he was just making a courtesy call.

Then, I remembered the part where I challenged Christ about being forsaken. Maybe, it just might be, could be, an issue to talk with him about. I was feeling a little uneasy about what I'd said.

He came in the next morning, fairly early. He had learned I'd be leaving for home later in the day and wanted to talk with me before I left. While he never actually stated it, I got the feeling he knew more about my ICU stay than I would have guessed.

A very nice, clean-cut, youthful-looking guy he was. If I would have met him on the street, I would never have seen him as a hospital chaplain. Because of his youthful appearance, my non-trusting mind quickly went to work. He's too young, *and healthy,* to know a whole lot about suffering and old age, probably knows a few ecumenical-sounding bible verses, and a few pat answers, but what could he really know about evil and suffering? I was already assuming this guy was a lightweight. (An old friend of mine had once asked me long ago, "What are the first three letters of the word assume?") I was here reminded of that rather quickly, it turned out.

He started out by asking a series of very casual-sounding questions. But, taken as a whole, I later realized, they were really good questions, as he was rather discreetly ascertaining my state of mind. After about an hour of talking, he seemed to visibly relax.

I finally realized that he had been worried about me doing myself bodily harm, so I came straight out and told him, "I would never harm myself." Pause.

"I would just kill myself and get it over with." Long, long pause. He was looking intently at me. Something in my face gave it away, and we both started laughing. Kind of like steam being released from a radiator.

In the process of talking with him, I gained more respect for him, and I began to feel idiot-like about my early wrong assumptions about him.

So, I told him what was bothering me.

I told him about the evening in the ICU when I had quit breathing and had thought that they were going to cut me open again. I told him that I'd been broken, and how I begged for death. All true.

But when I saw that wasn't going to happen and was powerless to do it myself, I became 'out of options'. Something hidden deep, deep, inside of me came welling up to the surface, brought by terror gone cosmic. What came to the surface, from my depths, was that I believed that all the suffering I was going through (and headed for more) was unfair.

I felt completely forsaken. God doesn't care. I'm forsaken.

How long, O Lord? Will you forget me forever? How long will you hide your face from me? How long shall I take counsel in my soul, having sorrow in my heart all day?

My addled, but terror-strafed mind drew me right to Christ's suffering on Calvary. It was then that Christ cried out, "My God, my God, why have you forsaken me?" And it was then, as I broke, nearly in two, that I rasped, "But you knew you weren't forsaken!"

The chaplain, for a while, just looked at me. Processing. *Long pause.* I told him I was feeling a bit guilty and a bit conflicted, maybe spiritually bereft for having challenged Christ in a not-very-servant-like way. A part of me wanted to forget it all and chalk it up to a nightmare, but I wanted to get his take on where I was.

Finally, he spoke.

"I deal, daily, with very angry people. Many are in the process of losing their faith or have already lost it, because of the pain and suffering they are going through. Sometimes, they even invite me to leave. They 'don't need' the likes of me."

Pause.

" But I'm not seeing that with you. What I am seeing is an honest question of why. "

Another pause. "In fact, I'm seeing, and feeling, no loss of faith at all."

I think it is commendable, in some ways. As far as challenging Christ goes, do not forget Calvary, and why He was there. He was there because of His great love for us. I think He can handle a challenge coming from one of His family."

My chaplain had gathered that I already understood that there is no easy, pat answer having to do with pain and suffering. And evil. He did proclaim his happiness (and relief, I suppose) that I was actually in a "very good spot," despite all my suffering. It's OK to ask why, he said because someday, we'll know. Sometimes we just have to wait for the answer.

As he left, he said, "May the Lord continue to bless you". He knew that, despite my pitiful physical condition, I heard and understood.

I couldn't help, at that moment, to remember the first three letters of the word assume.

CHAPTER 11

Coming Home

"He Has Risen"

On the 17th day, I came home.

It had been seventeen days since I first crawled into the ER, gasping for air. Eight days of star-aligning (getting the surgeons together amid Covid) along with prep/waiting. Followed by surgery and seven days in the ICU, and a night in my luxury hospital suite, I went home.

I should say, was brought home.

My sister-in-law, Jan, brought me home after spending all but one day in the hospital with me. She had been there since Day 2. I was in bad shape going in, I still don't remember how or when she found out, but once she did, she was there.

This was quite amazing to me, as she had a long way to drive to get there. But this heartwarming story had just begun.

Jan showed up the next morning, also, and announced that she would be my advocate. She meant it. Anybody that spends time in a hospital needs an advocate to help them understand, doctors, procedures, and choices. Most people are not fortunate enough to have one. I sure was. Jan was not only my advocate, but she stayed much of every day, as my visitor. Due to Covid, I could only have one visitor a day. This was huge. Hospitals can be very lonely and depressing places to live. Jan committed to every day except one. And on that day, my brother Mark came. They both spent an hour each day driving in the Front Range traffic crud. Talk about a tag team!

Most days she would talk with me, then do some texting for family updates, maybe read a book, or make some phone calls. Point is, she was always there, always ready to help with any new developments, either explaining or questioning them. Making sure I was getting cared for properly. A true Angel of Mercy. Plus, she kept a positive attitude toward what she knew was coming, suffering.

Being in a hospital for days, waiting for surgery, can be very depressing. She wouldn't let me go there, even though I tried. But because of her, I didn't. I had my down times, and fears cropping up constantly–she just brushed them aside with a "your-gonna-be-OK" attitude, and a reminder of how much better off I will be. Without Jan there, this whole ordeal would have been unbearable. With her there, I came away not only much better off, but forever in her debt. One that I could never, ever repay.

I was being helped into Jan's SUV. Trying to shield my eyes. So bright. And glorious. Oxygen tank clattering. Holes in my skin, and black, blue, green, and purple patterns all over my arms. Weakness in every appendage, every organ, in my brain.

Natural light invigorates me. I can do this.

I am home.

Wouldn't be, either, but Jan's gift keeps on giving. She has enlisted my nephew Joe to stay with me at night, open-ended. My sister, Jane, has offered to call on me every day, bringing me food, groceries, and recuperative love. Without these two great gifts, I would have ended up in rehab for 15-30 days. I have seen the inside of many rehab stations. Not a place I would willingly go to. Thank you, Jane and Joe.

I will never forget.

CHAPTER 12

New Beginning

I finally was able to inspect myself in the mirror. Up until now, I had only glanced a few times, then looked away. Pride hadn't let me look for long. I looked more like I had been in one of those camps where medical experiments had been conducted on the prisoners, and I had just barely survived. Hollow eyes, ghastly white color, drainage tubes hanging underneath my heart. Ugly scars, holes, and somebody else's chest. Emaciated, had lost 22 pounds. It looked like much of my skin was drooping; there was so much body missing.

But I was home, and what? I had to formulate a plan. Even though just thinking of trying to make any type of plan was like walking in quicksand. Slow, laborious, and sloppy. Since much of my brain was still missing, I had to give myself little speeches. *Don't give in. Your brain isn't working right, and neither is your body. Don't give in!* I knew intuitively that giving in would lead to depression. I guessed that, to fight it off, I would need some guerrilla warfare. *Keep moving or die.*

So, as soon as possible, I began to go on walks. At first, it was only around a very small block, dragging my oxygen canister, clinking and clattering behind me. That was all I could do.

Then, when I saw bits and pieces of my first sunrise through the trees and over the housetops, my clinking, and clattering began to sound like a Beethoven sonata. Then I began to feel like every new sunrise I saw gave me extra strength.

I knew it was going to be a long and arduous road back. But I had experienced so much love from my family and friends, that it had not only encouraged me, but it too, had strengthened me. Because of that, combined with the love of the Lord, I not only had to get better but had to achieve a state of thankfulness for what I had been carried through. This would take time, but I still had much to learn.

I admit to being a slow learner. Sometimes in the middle of the night, when the pain would keep me awake, I might angrily question the Lord, "why won't You get on with the healing, and how about some pain reduction? I'm hurting. And I can't sleep because of it." But I knew deep down, that going down that road was a fool's errand. A fool showing his weakness.

So, sunrise. Every morning. A reminder. Every morning. Even when sunrise was muted, it still spoke. Hope.

The Lord has not abandoned anybody. He has risen. It is only we, at times, that abandon Him.

Nobody ever said this was going to be easy.

When the storms are raging, stand by me.

CHAPTER 13

The First Night Home

I should have been in a rehab clinic.

But, because of the kindness and help I would receive from my family, I was allowed to stay at home. This meant a lot to me.

I have been to many rehab clinics, visiting friends and acquaintances, over the years. My experience is that they are generally understaffed, not really clean, and poorly run. I am sure not all are this way, but I had seen enough to know how fortunate I was that my sister-in-law, Jan, had enlisted my nephew Joe, to stay with me for the first few nights. And, to complete my salvation from the rehab clinic, my sister Jane would stop in on me during the day, bringing food, groceries, and recuperative love. This was actually the only way I could stay at home. Both Jane and Joe did these things willingly, and kindly. Both lived a long way away. *Bless their hearts, I am indebted to them forever.*

That first night was a strange one. I was really glad to be home, and frankly, after the rather long discharging process from the hospital, where I had never slept nearly as well as needed due to noises, groanings, blood tests, and opiate issues, I became ready for bed early. I was tired. I couldn't wait to be in my bed.

I knew getting into my bed wouldn't be easy. I had oxygen tubes in my nose and drainage tubes in my chest. As weak as I was, I think I even needed help getting into bed, all the tubes added more inconvenience. Being weak and cold, I asked Joe to put some heavy blankets on top of my usual spot. My own bed. Finally.

I'm home. I'm home! Ah-h-h-h-h-h. Sure felt good. "Good night, Joe, thanks again!"

As I lay there, I began to think. How long have I been gone? Six months, a year? It *seemed* a lifetime, which in a certain sense, it was.

When one is laying in a strange place, and suffering, time slowly-ever-so-slowly drips. *Drips to where?* Having no feeling for the actual time, as I had been strapped into lightless rooms, time took on a whole different meaning, a new, unquantifiable experience. Pain of width and depth unfathomable, on a scale unquantifiable. An enduring pain that accompanies every minute, that changes the face of a clock into a hanging Halloween pumpkin. I would say thank God for opiates, except that they generally delivered a pound of problems for every ounce of pain they masked. I had been in such a dungeon that it hadn't really occurred to me to try and keep track of time. My only real feel for time would occur every so often when I would involuntarily *twitch*. At that time, I had a bit of a feeling that something was moving along. On days when I was cognizant, Jan's coming and going had been my only real brush with time. But my brain was so crippled that I really never knew how many times she had actually come and gone.

How long *had* I been gone?

It was sixteen days. It was no small shock when I figured it out by looking at a calendar the next day.

My own bed!

Just before drifting off, I turned to get just a bit more comfortable. Well, I tried to turn. The blankets were so-o-o-o heavy. I could not turn. Felt like there was a 500-pound rhino sitting on me. I was pinned! I couldn't move my legs or hips. I never had a feeling like this before, helplessness coupled with a bit of claustrophobia. It seemed as if the blankets were now gaining weight. As if they were slowly, but inexorably working to crush me, even to flatten my brittle bones.

"Joe!", I rasped. "JOE!.... help!....HELP!" I was so weak I didn't know if he could hear me. But he did, thank God. He came and quickly pulled the heavies off me. The fear and the claustrophobia quickly subsided. But he knew what was coming, I could see it in his eyes. "Joe, I've got to sleep in my Lazy-Boy." He agreed with a "Let's go".

I slept in that Lazy-Boy for two months. It took me that long to screw up the courage to get back into my bed, which, for a while, I remembered as an Iron Mary.

CHAPTER 14

Cords

~

....the cords of death entangled me.....—(Psalm 18:4)

One of the aftereffects of my rather uncommon double surgery was a drop of oxygen in my blood. Neither my thoracic surgeon nor my cardio surgeon knew why this happened, and they were further stumped by the fact that I didn't seem to have any breathing problems that would *normally* accompany such a drop in oxygen. They both suggested that this *could* be a temporary situation, that it may have been a way the body was reacting to the severity of the surgical shock to the body. I had asked if I could do anything about it, such as exercise, and they both agreed–exercise couldn't hurt, and it may help. This is when I decided on a walking regimen, twice a day, initially to simply walk as far as I could.

Early on, this presented me with two problems. First, I was weak enough that walking *any* distance would be a challenge. But I figured that as soon as I got outdoors, in the sunshine, where I belonged, I would gain energy and strength just by being there. The second problem was the cords.

I was tethered to a portable oxygen concentrator in my house. I had cords that reached all over my house, which, at first, was a good thing because I could move around. But boy, they would *always* end up getting tangled, in a variety of ways. Sometimes the cord would get stuck on the corner of the table, sometimes on the corner of a chair leg, and *often* would get stuck on couch handles, and drawer handles (this was usually the most aggravating because this sticking was always accompanied by the cords in my nose being ripped out, sometimes painfully. The worst was when it would get caught *inside,* or under stools, or chairs. I would be moving one way, the cords another, and the cords in my nose another. Sometimes, this would have been comical if it hadn't been quite painful, and *really* irksome.

Luckily, I thought at the time, I had another oxygen container for when I left my house. I couldn't drive, but I used it for when anyone would take me to doctor's appointments. It was what I brought home with me from the hospital. About three feet tall, and weighing around 20 pounds, on wheels, it was my only chance to get in outdoor walking.

The first few nights in the Lazy Boy were a revelation. I discovered I could sleep fairly well in a chair, as it did lean back just far enough to be able to rest my head and keep my legs off the floor. The only problem was that I could never sleep for very long, as I would be woken up by pains in my chest. I could only take extra-strength Tylenol, which would work almost magically every night when I took it at bedtime. But, despite that, the pains in my chest would come and go, and be strong enough to wake me at night, sometimes feeling as if nerves were waking up; those were the sharp, but quick type. They would leave quickly. It was the other kind that would keep me awake, pushing right through and past the Tylenol.

The Ravitch is a complicated surgery. How does, or can, a surgeon break every bone in your chest, and then raise the whole chest off your organs, and then reset it (the chest) perfectly? I did not know it at the time, but the whole healing process in this condition was a crapshoot. Despite two titanium bars being inserted in my chest for stability, there is no way that anyone could know how well, and when, every bone would heal. If the bone will heal in the perfectly correct position, and how well each bone will heal about each other. I ended up with some very strange, but very real pains, that would last long enough to keep me awake for a while and concern me. You see, it felt like my *chest was moving*. And usually, it was a small, but painful part–a very small movement, but very noticeable. This led me to not only react to the pain but also to start feeling like I was going mad. This latest revelation was enough to keep me awake much longer than the pain lasted. At times I began to think that I was not only wrestling with a medical condition but that I was grappling with reality itself. Not good. I had been there before, most recently in the ICU. I did *not* want a repeat.

At this time, I started to feel, as a whole, *worse* than when I was in the hospital. Worse, because I had been expecting a miracle-quick recovery (I was so healthy, you see), and here I was, in worse shape, in some ways, than when I was in the hospital. I felt so weak *especially mentally* that I think I started a low-level panic that I had to fight off any way I could.

I began to feel as if I was forsaken, all over again. My prayer life quickly descended into impatience, requests for quick, almost miraculous, healing, and asking the Lord, "What good can come of me, sitting here day after day, night after night, doing little but suffering? I can't sleep through the night. I can't even go to the bathroom at night without having the cords ripped out of my nose, because I can't see what I'm doing! Every odd move I made sent another wave of pain throughout. What good am I doing anybody this way?"

How long, O Lord? Will you forget me
forever? How long will You hide Your face
from me? How long shall I take counsel
in my soul, having sorrow in my
heart all the day?
Psalm 13: 1-2

I was losing hope. It had only been a short time, but when one is suffering, with a lack of sleep, time drips by ever-so-slowly. Time soon came to a crawl. It was as if time itself became an entity and was going to great lengths to draw out my suffering. I'm too weak! I may not make it! And then the panic, which had been lower level, would rise a notch. But, sometimes, I might even get back to sleep, in exhaustion.

It was about then that the cords of death became the cords of life.

CHAPTER 15

The Sun Also Rises

~~~

Sleeping in the chair wasn't going to cut it. A few mornings of waking up and looking straight into my kitchen was a bit disconcerting. However, not wanting to even get out of the chair was even more so. Hiding under my covers, with only my head showing, I stared. My eyes shifted to the clock, then back to straight ahead–the kitchen. Never one to be hungry early, I wondered how long I would stare at my nice, small little kitchen before I would work up an appetite. This was an empty endeavor. Sitting around, under blankets, wondering about eating long before I ever eat? I had just woken up, and I was already grab-bagging, trying to create a purpose *to do anything.*

I couldn't wait until the morning.

I then looked at my oxygen canister, sitting there, looking stupid and useless. Yeah, but at least it had a purpose......*wait a minute! That's it! I'm gonna go for a walk! If it kills me, I don't care.* I *have* to *do* something. I maneuvered my way out of the chair and blankets, found some walking shoes and a coat, and got rid of my cords of death. This, along with a visit to the bathroom, seemed to take hours.

With my mobile concentrator, the cords were a constant aggravating reminder of my prison. I could not go anywhere with them, other than around my house, pinching, snagging, and annoying much of the time. But my canister, this was my ticket to freedom. THESE cords would bring me life! I could walk outside; something I hadn't done in many days since I first had crawled into the ER. The surgeons had told me exercise was good. However much I could do without too much stress was the goal. I will attempt to walk again!

With much difficulty, I finally made it out my front door. Still trying to figure out if it was easier to push it or to pull it. This was no small accomplishment. It took me a while to realize pulling the heavy canister would work best. But I was free! I could walk! Not very far, but I could walk. Already tired from dressing myself, and getting my gear through the door, I made a modest goal of simply walking around the block for my first effort. I did. The trees and houses obscured the sunrise, so, on my first trip I saw very little. Besides, I was gassed by the time I got home. It probably took me almost half an hour. Today, that same walk would take me about three minutes, as the block I live on is very small and short.

But, as tired as I was while walking, I did manage to catch a glimpse, not directly of the sunrise, but of the eastern sky it lit up. Something then happened. I stopped myself and my canister. And stood there for just a second. First, I felt a surge of adrenaline, which at this time, was *really enjoyable.* And this caused another sensation within me. Though at the time, I had no idea why. There it was, an honest-to-God long, shiny ray of hope, welling up within me. Where did that come from? A few short hours ago I had felt utterly forsaken, with unanswered prayer feeling like a long depression lurking. I may have been gassed when I got back, but I already couldn't wait for tomorrow morning.

CHAPTER 16

The Sun Also Rises

My first sunrise in the new world.

A difficult night. I had gone through enough pain that I was awake more than normal. When one lies awake at night, there is more than just pain, and weakness to deal with. At least for me. Feeling like I was forsaken, or at least forgotten about, I started to descend into a pit of loneliness. Not just a home-alone type of loneliness, but a cosmic left-to-suffer alone loneliness that seeped into my very core. While I knew that my redeemer lives, in the dark of the night that seemed to never end, it felt to me that He had become MIA.

Where are you, Lord? Why are you so far from me? You do not despise me, do you? Then why do I sit here, hour after hour, with my mind leading me into a chamber of horrors? The physical pain isn't even the worst! My mind is even weaker than my body, and it tells me that I am approaching a type of abyss as if walking toward a cliff—and being helpless not to fall off? Where are you? Where *are You?*

This complaint, amidst others, almost lasted till dawn, but not quite.

I awoke with a start.

Well, there's my kitchen. Here are my cords. Here's my blanket. No abyss, yet. I looked toward my south windows, partially shaded. There it was, just the barest sliver of light. Time to get up and go! Only this time, I was going to walk another block further east, where I could get out and see *the* sunrise. It had been so long since I'd seen one—used to see them almost every morning, probably taking them mostly for granted—yesterday, for some reason, was an exciting hint. Still didn't know why.

Finally made it into the clear. *Two blocks—lotta work!* The horizon had a thin, horizontal line of blood-red for as far as my eye could see, both north and south. The next layer of color, directly on top of the first layer, was a beautiful layer of orange, bronco orange, much thicker with shades of orange lightening as your eyes went higher. This was followed by the barest hint of a line of royal blue, with a large and long dish of pastel blue reaching heavenward.

I say 'dish' because, frankly, I just sat there drinking it in, Maybe slurping it up would be a better picture. I think I even closed my eyes for a minute or two, letting the light settle on my face as if it were a nurturing skin cream being applied. When I re-opened my eyes, I felt as though I were enmeshed *in the sunrise itself.* As if I had *absorbed* it.

I just stood there for a while, probably grinning, probably looking stupid to anyone passing by. *(Glad there wasn't anybody)* But the wait had been worth it. I resolved then and there that I would never take another sunrise for granted. Whether it be the beauty provided by the Great Artist, or it be the simple fact of being able to see one at all because I had missed so many. Whether it be the life (and healing) it had just breathed into me, it didn't matter. All these things were something I would not, could not, ever take lightly again.

But, what about this hope-y thing? Where did *that* come from, I wondered, as I slowly made my way back home, the two blocks seeming much shorter, now. *Poof!*

It popped back into my brain as if it had been let out at one time for a trip to the coast. Of course! The sun rises. The Son rose, a Christian symbol of hope. There's a reason why every Easter, there are sunrise services literally all over the world.

From the darkness, the sun rises to feed, nourish, and warm the earth. From a tomb, the son rose, to save the world. What a great time for a reminder, just about the time I was losing hope that my recovery would be anything but misery, or even that I'd recover. I did not know it yet, but once I resolved never to take a sunrise for granted again, it got even more interesting.

I resolved never to take another sunrise for granted.

CHAPTER 17

From Across the Universe

A couple more mornings of walking to the edge of my townhome development, and back. A couple more days of getting stronger. I was still tethered to my oxygen day and night, but at least I felt a bit better, and mentally, the cloud was starting to clear. Still, the nights were difficult.

Sometimes it was simply shifting a little in my chair, and *zap*, a sharp pain would zip through my chest, often unable to pinpoint where the pain originated. This would wake me for quite some time, for, even if the pain went away, I was still angry from being woken in this way. While acknowledging that I *may* be improving a little, my prayers were still essentially whined, as in "How long, O Lord, will you forget me forever?" *If the Psalmist could question Him this way, then why not me?*

Rays of light, at times, look like
heavenly searchlights.

I heard a voice from heaven
like the sound of many waters
and like the sound of thunder...
Revelation 14:2

About this time, I resolved to walk further in the morning. There was a golf course two blocks away, and easy access to the north side of it, just across from where I lived. I really needed to get there. I missed golf so much, and at this juncture, was wondering if I'd ever golf again. I needed to be on a golf course with the sun coming up, inhaling its rarified air, dreaming of well-struck wedges sticking near the pin.

Really excited to make the trip, I clinked and clattered onto a maintenance road for about fifty yards, and there I was: breathing golf course oxygen. While there were some threatening clouds in the east, the muted sunrise brought an artistic bonus: rays of light, sneaking through some of the clouds. At times, seeming like heavenly searchlights, but a minute later looking like golden beams only one Artist could draw. I started to smile. *Maybe He's looking for me. He sure doesn't seem to know where I live.*

I heard what I thought was a rumble out of the east, interrupting a nice little daydream I was having about knocking one over this lake I was approaching. But something was amiss. There were some dark clouds, surely, but this sound I heard wasn't really a rumble. It sounded more like a voice, or voices, way far off, too far off to be intelligible. There was another one, closer! This time I could tell, a voice–or voices coming together. Only one way I could get *near* describing this: Rev. 14–" like the sound of many waters, and thunder!"

Boom!

It was right over my head, coming from the clouds above me!

For some reason, I was not frightened at all; just *very* interested in what was happening.

Thundering: "Where were you when I laid the foundation of the earth? Tell me, if you have an understanding. Have you ever in your life commanded the morning? And caused the dawn to know its place? "

Where were you when I laid the
foundation of the earth? Tell Me,
if you have understanding…
Have you ever in your life commanded
the morning, and caused the dawn
to know its place?
Job 38: 4, 12

49

It would seem that I should have been terrified, but I was more giddy than anything. Yes! Yes! I get it. I will whine no more.

This was only the start.

The next morning, noise of a different sort, a beautiful melody swept into my ears, and then, just for a second or two, perched in my brain: *little darlin', it's been a long cold lonely winter. Here comes the sun.*

Little darlin', it's been a long, cold lonely winter… Here comes the sun.
The Beatles, Here Comes the Sun

Not caring, at this point, if anyone would question my veracity or sanity, I pressed on. Logic? Reason? Incredulity? Believe whatever your pre-suppositions tell you to. I'm going back to school, and my skull full of mush is being taught by Mr. Sunrise.

A few mornings later, I was clattered by a small, placid lake. Softly, softly, it came.

I heard no voice, but it kept coming: *He leads me beside quiet waters, He restores my soul.* This also soothed my wounded heart, can't explain how.

He leads me beside quiet waters, He restores my soul.

I was getting excited, just to go. For a short time, I started to wake up earlier and leave earlier. I soon found myself, in the dark, near the lake, with only a sliver of light on the horizon. While it was a beautiful red-orange, there wasn't much of it.

It was dark enough that I almost tripped over something I could not see. It was then that Emily Dickinson sent me a message, by what medium I can't say: *I am out with lanterns, looking for myself.* She attached a P.S. a few days later when I walked for a long time into a sunrise that started with only a sliver but got to the point, ever so slowly, with an orange-yellow-then-azure-blue symphony of color:

The truth must dazzle gradually, or every man be blind.

The truth must dazzle gradually, or every man be blind…
Emily Dickinson

There were sunrises so beautiful–almost too beautiful for words, but the melody of How Great Thou Art found its way in *Thy art, throughout the universe displayed…*

Thy art, throughout the universe, displayed.

How Great Thou Art

As enjoyable as school was, there were some really dark periods. Because of how I felt, most days dripped by slowly. Not just the pain and weakness, but the never-ending oxygen companion. At times aggravating and always annoying, and I was constantly trying to ignore it, never really succeeding. I often felt a real weariness, not just bodily, but deep into my soul. Sometimes walking early would exacerbate the problem. If it was dark enough, I might have started to inadvertently taken a slightly different path and pass through an unfamiliar spot. Dante's *Divine Comedy* leaped right off the stage: *In the middle of my life, I found myself in a dark wood, for the straightway was lost.* If this weariness lasted for more than a day, I would, at times, get this strange feeling that something good was coming out of it: *The long and winding road, that leads to your door.*

Shadows from sunrises could be really interesting, sometimes a lesson in themselves. Once I came to a fork in the road, and looking back, noticed an interesting shadow from my ugly canister. I was almost immediately visited by a very old friend, Robert Frost, whom I hadn't heard from in quite a long time: *Two roads diverged in a yellow wood, and, I took the one less traveled by.*

Two roads diverged in a yellow wood, and, I took the one less traveled.
Robert Frost

Once, in the very early hour, I saw a rather large shadow, its shape being ominous looking, I know not why. So, William Shakespeare calmly and evenly sheds light: *This life, which had been a tomb of his virtue and honor, is but a walking shadow.*

I arrived later than usual one dark and forbidding morning. There was a serious storm headed my way, and off to the south I saw a huge, touching-the-ground cloudbank, which looked to be a quarter of a mile long, about four stories high, slowly and very menacingly moving toward me. Ponderous, but scary looking enough to calculate when to make the turn homeward. The book of Job came oozing: *Can you draw out Leviathan with a fishhook? Can you put a rope in his nose? Or pierce his jaw with a hook? Will he make supplications to you? Or will he speak to you with soft words?*

Can you draw out Leviathan with
a fishhook? Can you put a
rope in his nose? Or pierce his jaw
with a hook? Will he make many
supplications to you? Or will he speak
to you with soft words?

Job 41: 1-3

It made no difference to me that this monster was mythological. Calamity was stalking. I was out of there.

But even on the darkest of days, there was always hope. I would often go back to the reality of it all, that this Sun, from millions of miles away, both directly and indirectly was the catalyst and nurturer of all life. And healer, too. This was *personal.* An impersonal God would never heal. We were visited by a *person* 2000 years ago, a *person* who showed His love for us, by what He did, while *here.* An impersonal God would never love because an impersonal God cannot love. And yet, we are constructed in such a way, that love is the most important thing in every life. Love is no accident, otherwise, it would only be an illusion. Go figure.

And the book of Matthew often would bring this home: *For He causes his sun to rise on the evil and the good.*

I had two more surgeries, the first one not so bad–the two titanium bars planted in my reconstructed chest (for stability) were being taken out, and the very next morning I got out of the hospital, walked fifteen blocks home by myself, in my new portable oxygen backpack. Piece of cake. I was walking early the next morning, and could not stop it: *Sun's comin' up, I got cakes on the griddle...*

Sun's comin' up, I got cakes on the griddle...
John Denver

The fourth surgery, however, was a bear. A painful recovery in the worst of places. But there was Willa Cather, all one hundred pounds of wisdom, making sure I that I wouldn't dwell for too long in the pain:

> *Ruin and new birth; the shudder of ugly things in the past,*
>
> *the trembling image of beautiful ones on the horizon;*
>
> *finding and losing, that was life.*

Ruin and new birth;
the shudder of
ugly things in the past, the trembling
image of beautiful ones on the horizon;
finding and losing, that was life.

Willa Cather, *The Pioneer Women's Story*

She, among others, was helping me mend. The school was the sunrise, they were the teachers, teaching what the Superintendent had taught *them.* Charles Dickens had one last class, just about the time the suffering had almost dissipated, the air was warmer, and the sunrises coming ever so early. I felt like I was nearing graduation.

I have been bent and broken–
I hope into a better shape.
Charles Dickens

CHAPTER 18

My First Sunrise

❧

Late in the spring, about the time I was feeling much more human and a lot healthier. I started out on my early morning walk with a feeling of well-being. As in, *this ain't so bad.* My health was improving, and even my minute-by-minute aggravation with the oxygen had been reduced greatly. My oxygen numbers had improved enough to where I needed oxygen only on my walks and while I was sleeping (sleep apnea). I had traded in my large, noisy, unwieldy, cantankerous oxygen canister for a smaller, much lighter container that I could carry as a backpack. By this time, I believed that I would soon be oxygen-free. None of my doctors or surgeons could tell me *why* I had the condition, so I figured that all my work, especially walking, had as good a chance as anything in improving me, until I no longer needed to depend on my oxygen tank. I could see this day coming, all was good.

Such was my frame of mind when I walked straight into a blinding sunrise that morning, in a place where there were only a few small trees to shield my eyes from the brilliance of the sun. Suddenly, from somewhere among the small trees, an old familiar song sang out to me: *Doo-doo doodle-loot doot-doo.* Stunningly clear, close, and oh-so-beautiful. I could not see him, but I knew an old friend had come back, to a place where I had never seen or heard meadowlarks before. I could not see him, but it mattered not. He even gave me an encore" *Doo-doo doodle-loot doot-doo.*

I started walking very slowly. I started to drift a little. I may have even come to a stop. Drifting. The song, combined with the brilliant, blinding sun drifted me all the way back to childhood. Magical.

I was told the sun was far, far away,
but this morning, it seemed right next to me.

I have heard enough psychological talk about "happy places" in one's childhood to understand that this can be of some importance. A few years ago, a friend asked me "where" my happy place was. I had to think about it, long and hard. "I didn't have one," I groused. I think the reply saddened her, which saddened me.

It was truthful but inaccurate. I just needed a memory jog.

I did not have an unhappy childhood. I don't believe I was mistreated, so I never had to concern myself with excuses for any of my failures in life.

However, my childhood wasn't all that happy, either.

A middle child in a family of ten children. Our home was a cauldron of motion.

Kid energy, neurotic energy, creative energy, humorous energy. Sometimes a blur, sometimes slapstick, sometimes slow-motion, but always there.

In that milieu, I tended to get lost. An uncle once called me, "the quiet one," which, in my lineage, may have loosely translated into "the stupid one." Not sure, but the main thing is that I really never felt part of the flow. At times, I felt like I was in the way of *everyone else's flow*. It didn't help that my mother, who had her hands full with at least six or seven other children at any given time, would say, "you're in the way, move!' Another one which *had* to be a German idiom, that was loosely translated, caused me no end of reflection was, "wake up and die right!"

I remember trying, at various times, my hand at being the Family Jester, just looking for a little attention. This endeavor had mixed results. So mixed, in fact, that one of my brothers called me a masochist. When he first said the word masochist, I think I had to look it up in the dictionary.

But I did have a happy place, as it turns out. It had been buried by time and history. I just needed something, or someone, to dig it out of me. And come it did, by way of a beautiful poem written by my brother. When I first read this great piece of poetry (found in the Epilogue), this happy place came *immediately* to my frontal lobes, and then slowly slid into my heart. I remember getting a bit emotional.

On this fine morning, this beautiful meadowlark (not seen but heard) had brought me back. I drifted back easily.

I had to get outside early most mornings, if possible. When I could, the weather being decent, I would wander to different places in our huge yard, or empty lot next door. Abutted up against our property was a fairground, with barns, a long racetrack, and a grandstand. There was a little field between the barns and the racetrack, and I found myself heading there one fine morning. This was illegal, as I had been told never to go "down there" by myself, but the sirens called. I had heard the meadowlarks from near my back door. To me, they were performing a concerto, and I didn't even know what a concerto was, but I just *had* to get closer and hear.

Hear more, hear better.

As I headed through a forbidden gate, I thought, *"could this be my garden of Eden?"*

The sun was almost up, sitting huge and blinding on the spring horizon. I had been told the sun was far, far away, but this morning it felt like it was right next to me. Blinding to look at, warming on the skin, illuminating the field I was in the midst of, and *coloring*. Dandelions everywhere, large and thick, almost like a yellow-golden rug. It seemed this brilliant sun that I could not look at, was reflecting, softly, the dandelion colors back to me, almost as if they were little extensions of the sun's rays darting about.

I was in a rosy, golden state, dreamlike. For a minute or so, I felt like I was home. A place where I smiled, all by myself, all too myself. A place to just *be.*

Looking for meadowlarks. I could still hear them, some far off, but many closer, some real close. With their yellow breasts and brown necklaces, they blended right into the taller dandelions, but they kept right on singing. As I kept moving, some would go silent.

And then I saw him. Perched on the racetrack fence, huge for a meadowlark, this beautiful yellow-breasted, brown-necklaced soloist stood by himself. He stared at me. I took a step or two closer, then stopped, not wanting to scare him away. He opened his mouth. *Doo-doo doodle-loot doot-doo!* Right at me! He was singing to me. He was singing....to me!

I had to go and make an introduction. I liked talking to animals then, and I still do now but of course, as soon as I got within twenty feet of him, he flew off. I waved at him, actually hoping I'd see him again. Sigh. I knew I wouldn't. I stayed there for a long time, happy to be well, *happy.* In the here, and now. There and then.

I had almost come to a stop. I just then realized I had a lot more walking to do.

The healing was darn near complete, or so I felt.

Epilogue

I owe my brother a debt of gratitude for his
poem not only jogging my memory back into
my "happy place", but for the beauty (both
sight and sound) of the poem itself, and for
the permission to present it below:

Meadowlark
O Meadowlark! Bold and bright!
Angelic tan and yellow sprite!
Sing once more of joy unbridled!
When your soul's sweet melody pierces the air
All creatures stand in silence, blessed to hear!

For the One that fills you all in all,
Even your voice, so enthralling, so enthralled,
So often proves to be far too great,
And this is why you sing. Although it seems
Your heart must burst, sing! And render all to Him!

Meadowlark, rehearse again your native blend,
Blithely unaware that men are fallen
Far from natural joys, go and fill the skies
With raptured calls and effortless harmonies,
Then come and teach your perfect song to me!

Mark Ziegler, *Wordsongs*

Bio

Born in the heat of the summer in North Dakota to Conrad and Ann Ziegler, Conrad (Jr.) was a middle child in a family of ten children. Enjoyed books and sports early, his proudest moment in early life was when he received his Library Card at age 6. Conrad migrated to Colorado at age 17, where he has lived ever since. His early involvement in the hotel business there led him directly into the wine industry, where he managed a retail wine business for twenty years, and owned it for ten years. Conrad has enjoyed books his whole life, with history, theology, poetry, and sports his main interests. He is retired and enjoys golf, chess, and urban hikes. Four surgeries in a six month period that changed his body, mind, and soul also left him with a desire to write about some of his trials and tribulations, and interesting people along the way. He enjoys talking with animals.

www.ingramcontent.com/pod-product-compliance
Lightning Source LLC
LaVergne TN
LVHW061330060426
835513LV00015B/1346